Disney

101 DALMATIANS

Level 3

Re-told by: Marie Crook
Series Editor: Rachel Wilson

Pearson Education Limited
KAO Two
KAO Park, Harlow,
Essex, CMI7 9NA, England
and Associated Companies throughout the world.

ISBN: 978-1-2923-4674-8

This edition first published by Pearson Education Ltd 2020

1 3 5 7 9 10 8 6 4 2

Heinemann Roman Special, 14pt/23pt
Printed by Neografia, Slovakia

Published by Pearson Education Limited

Acknowledgments
123RF.com: Katherine Bernard Yip-Choy 24, soundsnaps 23
Alamy Stock Photo: Juniors Bildarchiv GmbH 26
Getty Images: Wesley Martinez Da Costa / EyeEm 22
Shutterstock.com: Arsenie Krasnevsky 24, Grigorita Ko 26-27,
Helga Madajova 24, MBI 22, Reddogs 24

For a complete list of the titles available in the Pearson English Readers series, visit
www.pearsonenglishreaders.com.

Alternatively, write to your local Pearson Education office or
to Pearson English Readers Marketing Department,
Pearson Education, KAO Two, KAO Park, Harlow, Essex, CMI7 9NA

In This Book

Roger
A kind man from London

Anita
A kind woman from London

Pongo
Roger's Dalmatian dog

Perdita
Anita's Dalmatian dog

Cruella De Vil
Anita's old classmate

Sergeant Tibs
A helpful cat

Before You Read

Introduction

101 Dalmatians is a story about Roger and Anita. They fall in love and their dogs fall in love, too. They have a lot of puppies. They are a happy family. Then the terrible Cruella De Vil comes to call …

. . . .

Activities

1 **Look at the pictures in the story, then read the sentences. Say Yes or No.**

1 A Dalmatian is a white dog with black spots.
2 There are two Dalmatians in this story.
3 Cruella De Vil is very kind.
4 There are some puppies in this story.

2 **Look at the pictures on pages 12 and 13. Say the things you can see.**

1 A cat
2 A puppy
3 A fur coat
4 A park
5 A truck

Roger and his Dalmatian dog Pongo live in London. Every day, Pongo looks out of the window, bored and a little sad. Pongo wants to have a family one day. He wants Roger to have one, too.

One day, Roger takes Pongo for a walk in the park. They meet Anita and Perdita there. Anita is a beautiful woman and Perdita is her beautiful Dalmatian dog. Roger smiles at Anita and Pongo smiles at Perdita.

Roger and Anita fall in love. They are very happy.

Pongo and Perdita are also in love. They want to start a family.

They would like to have some puppies.

Some weeks later, fifteen puppies arrive! Pongo and Perdita are very happy.

Then one day, they hear a car outside. *Beeep!* "Oh, Pongo … it's her! It's that terrible woman!" cries Perdita. She doesn't like Anita's old classmate, Cruella De Vil.

Cruella is wearing her fur coat. She loves fur and she loves the Dalmatians' beautiful coats. "Where are the puppies?" she asks Anita, "I would like to buy them all! Today!" Cruella smiles a terrible smile.

Cruella wants a new fur coat—white with black spots.
"Oh, no," Roger says. "You can't buy the puppies.
They're our family."
Cruella is very angry. She wants the puppies and she
has an idea.

The next evening, Roger and Anita take Pongo and Perdita
for a walk to the park. The puppies stay at home.
Two bad men are waiting outside. They see Roger and Anita
leave and they go into the house.

Roger and Anita come back … and the puppies are not there.
"We have to get help," Pongo tells Perdita. They go to the park
and they bark and bark. They are calling for help.

Some animals in the country hear their call and they start to look for the puppies. Sergeant Tibs the cat says, "I remember hearing a noise at the old De Vil house. Perhaps it's the puppies!" They go over to Cruella's old house and look inside.

Back in London, Pongo and Perdita are very sad.
Then they hear a dog barking outside. "Listen! There's some
news about the puppies!" says Pongo. That night, they jump
through a window and run to the park. They speak to a friend.

"We know where your puppies are," he says.

"They're at Cruella De Vil's house in the country."

"Cruella De Vil!" Pongo and Perdita cry. Suddenly,
they understand. "We have to go NOW!" Pongo says.

Tibs the cat sees the puppies through Cruella's window.
He starts to count them—"13, 14, 15 …" he says. He knows they're
Pongo and Perdita's puppies. Suddenly, he stops and listens.

Cruella is talking to the two bad men.

"I want my Dalmatian coat tonight!" she shouts.

Tibs jumps through the window and into the house.

"Come on!" he tells the puppies. "It's time to get out of here."

Suddenly, Pongo and Perdita arrive. They see their puppies.
They see a lot of puppies! 16, 17, 18, 19, 20 … and more! Pongo
and Perdita jump at the men. Tibs helps the puppies outside.

Tibs says goodbye and the puppies run into the cold, dark night. Pongo and Perdita follow them through the snow and Cruella and the men follow in their cars. The Dalmatians run faster than the cars!

The Dalmatians find a small village and they hide in an
old building. It's very dirty in there, but Pongo has an idea.
"Play in the dirt, puppies!" he says.
They are very surprised! "We can get dirty! *Hooray!*"

Quickly they understand. Now their coats are not white with black spots. The Dalmatians are black dogs now!
They jump into a truck. Cruella sees only black dogs. But one puppy gets wet and suddenly Cruella can see the spots.

"Catch them!" Cruella cries. She is very angry.
The truck starts to leave with the Dalmatians in the back.
Cruella and the two bad men drive dangerously through the
snow. They go faster and faster and faster and then they *crash*!

Roger and Anita are very sad. They are waiting for Pongo and Perdita to come home with their puppies.

Suddenly, the door opens and Pongo, Perdita, and a lot of very dirty and very excited puppies run into the room!

Roger and Anita count the dogs. "101 Dalmatians!" they cry.
"What can we do with all these puppies?" Anita asks.
Roger smiles. "They can stay," he says. "We can be one big,
happy family! One *very* big, happy family!"

After You Read

1 **Look at the pictures in the story and find:**

1 Pongo and Perdita sleeping
2 Pongo walking
3 Tibs the cat sitting
4 Cruella smiling
5 Puppies getting dirty

2 **Read and say Yes or No.**

1 A puppy is a baby cat.
2 Anita loves fur coats.
3 Two bad men take the puppies to Cruella De Vil's house.
4 Pongo and Perdita find their puppies.
5 There are 107 puppies in this story.

3 **Match the sentences to the characters.**

1 She likes fur coats.
2 They have 15 puppies.
3 He is a cat.
4 She loves Roger.
5 They take the puppies
to Cruella's house.

a Cruella
b Tibs
c The two bad men
d Pongo and Perdita
e Anita

Picture Dictionary

classmate

fall in love

fur

bark

hide

inside

outside

puppy

spot

snow

crash

village

Phonics

Say the sounds. Read the words.

ar — car — park

ir — bird — dirty

or — bored — horse

ur — fur — hurt

Say the rhyme.

Birds in the park.
A horse in the dark.
A dog with curly fur
Starts to bark.

Values

Protect your friends.

Find Out

How much do you know about dogs?

Dogs are the world's favorite pet. They can see and smell very well. They can hear much better than people can. They love to go for walks.

Do you know?

- Chocolate makes dogs sick.
- Smaller dogs often live longer than bigger dogs.
- Some dogs have short fur. Some have long fur.
- A dog's fur is called a "coat."
- There are over 340 kinds of dog.

smell you use your nose to smell things
size how big or small a thing is